My Favorite Machines

Motorcycles

Colleen Ruck

A$^+$

Smart Apple Media

Smart Apple Media
P.O. Box 3263, Mankato, MN 56002

 An Appleseed Editions book

Planning and production by Discovery Books Limited
Designed by D.R ink
Edited by Colleen Ruck

Library of Congress Cataloging-in-Publication Data

Ruck, Colleen.
 Motorcycles / by Colleen Ruck.
   p. cm. -- (My favorite machines)
 Includes index.
 ISBN 978-1-59920-676-9 (library binding)
1. Motorcycles--Juvenile literature. I. Title.
TL440.15.R83 2012
 629.2275--dc22
                          2011010387

Photograph acknowledgments:
Discovery Photolibrary: p. 17; Getty Images: p. 9 (Tilmann schlootz); Honda News: pp. 7, 13; Kawasaki: p. 12; Library of Congress: 8; Shutterstock: pp. 5 (Robert Kelsey), 6 (Ljupco Smokovski), 11 (Harsanyi Andras), 14, 15 (Ljupco Smokovski), 18 (Chen wei seng), 19 (Tan Kian Khoon), 20 (Tiut Lucian), 21, 22 (Margo Harrison), 23; Suzuki: p. 4; Wikimedia: p. 16; Yamaha: p. 10.

Printed in the United States of America at Corporate Graphics
In North Mankato, Minnesota

DAD0502
52011

9 8 7 6 5 4 3 2 1

Contents

Motorcycles Everywhere 4

Controls 6

Early and Classic Bikes 8

Superbikes 10

Touring Bikes 12

Customized Bikes 14

Scooters 16

Track Bikes 18

Off-road Bikes 20

Stunt Riding 22

Glossary and Web sites 24

Index 24

Motorcycles Everywhere

Motorcycles are two-wheeled motor **vehicles**. Some bikes are for everyday use.

Other bikes are designed for off-road racing.

Controls

Riders control the brakes with their hands and feet.

Clutch: for changing gear

Gear change pedal

The rider twists the **throttle** to go faster.

Throttle

Early and Classic Bikes

This is an early motorcycle from the 1900s.

Early motorcycles looked like a bicycle with an **engine**.

Some people collect
classic bikes like this
1930 Indian motorcycle.

Superbikes

Superbikes are the fastest and most powerful bikes on the road. A superbike engine is as powerful as a car engine!

Motorcycle racers lean with the bike when they ride fast around corners.

Touring Bikes

Touring bikes are the biggest motorcycles. They are designed to cover long distances.

Storage box

Heated handgrips

This bike has a place to store **luggage,** and the seats and handgrips can be heated.

Customized Bikes

Some bike owners like to change the way their bike looks. This bike has colorful paint that makes it stand out from the crowd.

This custom bike is called a chopper. It looks cool with its low seat and high handlebars.

Scooters

Scooters are smaller, less powerful motorcycles. They are easy and comfortable to ride. The engine is under the seat.

A policeman directs scooters in the city of Rome, Italy.

People often use scooters for short trips in cities.

Track Bikes

Motorcycle racing is a fast and exciting sport.

Racing bike riders wear a tough helmet and a thick leather suit with kneepads.

Off-road Bikes

Some motorbikes are ridden off-road. They are built for driving on rough, muddy ground.

In motocross, riders race around a hilly track jumping over ramps, dips, and hills.

Stunt Riding

Stunt riders perform tricks and jumps on their bikes.

This is a trials bike. Riders have to race round a dangerous **obstacle** course without falling off.

Glossary

engine	Part of a vehicle that gives it power to move.
designed	Made for the job.
luggage	Bags and suitcases you take with you when traveling somewhere.
obstacle	Something that is in the way so you have to ride over or around it.
perform	To do a show in front of a crowd.
throttle	Found on the handlebar, the throttle increases the speed of the bike when it is twisted.
vehicle	A machine, often with an engine, which moves people or goods from one place to another.

Web sites

http://auto.howstuffworks.com/motorcycle.htm
Find out how motorbikes work.

www.tmxnews.co.uk/website_content/bikes
Introduction to the various off-road motorcycling competitions.

www.totalmotorcycle.com
This website is packed full of photographs, with the latest motorbike models and lots more.

Index

chopper 15
classic bikes 9
controls 6-7
crashes 19
customized bikes 14-15

early bikes 8
engine 8, 10, 16

motocross 21

off-road bikes 5, 20-21

paint 14

racing 11, 18-19, 21, 23

scooters 16-17
stunt riding 22-23
superbikes 10-11

touring bikes 12-13
trials bikes 23